Breaking Into Breakout Boxes:
Escape Rooms in Education

Holly Elizabeth Johnson

DEDICATION

I dedicate this book to my precious children, Dixie and Nicholas. I never dreamed that two little people could make my life so rich and full of joy. May the Lord bless you and keep you and may all your dreams come true.

CONTENTS

ACKNOWLEDGMENTS

First and foremost, this book would not have even been a thought in my wildest dreams had it not been for the woman who pioneered breakout boxes at my school and accepted the challenge of, "I don't know what I'm doing or how I'm doing it, but the students will love it, so here it goes." I will be eternally grateful and indebted to Sarah Beth Henderson - thank you for being a leader and an innovative teacher.

Secondly, I want to thank my mother. When I half-jokingly told her that I should write a book for all the educators who had not heard of this incredible resource called breakout boxes with which teachers could effectively engage their students, she immediately told me to start writing. As an educator herself, she knew that teachers wanted an easy-to-use approach to one of the most innovative ideas in education and a resource that could be duplicated for immediate use in the classroom. She has been an invaluable sounding board and awesome editor. She has always been my biggest cheerleader and most avid fan. I couldn't have done it without you, Mom. You have <u>always</u> been the wind beneath my wings.

Finally, I want to thank my husband. Even though he doubted there was a market for the book (which remains to be seen) and had no idea what I was mumbling about or counting at ten o'clock at night in front of the computer, he always encouraged me. He listened to me prattle on about clues with which he was unfamiliar and watched the kids so I could work obsessively to finish. His love and support made this book possible more than my enthusiasm for the subject matter.

So without further ado, let's break into some boxes!

1

What is a Breakout Box?

Nothing prompts my students to come to school or turn in assignments as the promise of a breakout box. It is the magic wand that excites students to interact with targeted subject material and spurs them to work harder than normal. Not only that, but it encourages students with different learning styles to collaborate with every student working on the project. Why is that? My theory is that the promise of reward, bragging rights, and the excitement of each opening lock generates that intrinsic motivation that educators so often seek when assigning work. This is what it is......

What is it?!

Have you ever heard of an escape room? Similar concept - in reverse. Instead of trying to break OUT of a locked room, students are trying to break IN to a box with a series of locks on it. Never heard of an escape room? It's a locked room that holds a

1

group of paying customers who must solve a series of clues in order to escape before the time runs out. For a breakout box, the teacher hides clues around the classroom each of which, when correctly solved, opens one of the locks on the box. Each of the clues are skills or concepts in the subject area that are made in such a way that they provide a combination to one of the locks. For example, if students are learning about important dates in history, a clue could be four important events and the dates they occurred listed on a piece of paper, with one digit from the date omitted. When students find (or remember) the missing digit in the date, the four missing numbers would be the combination to open one of the locks!

I usually create a box with five locks and a sixth lock on a separate box that contains something else inside. There are companies who sell the entire "kit" - the box with all the locks, but you can make your own from Amazon for much cheaper. The locks I like to use are a 3-digit lock, a four-digit lock, a directional lock, a word lock and a key lock (I will explain all of the locks in detail in chapter 2). It is important that the locks are different so that the students are not confused about which clue opens which lock (although they will be anyway!). You can use more locks, fewer locks, different locks - once you get used to the concept of the breakout box, you can change it up to match your subject matter.

The basic premise is this: students have 45 minutes to solve all of the clues to open the locks to the breakout box. The teacher hides the clues around the classroom and students have to find and solve the clues to open the locks. I divide the students into teams, usually 2 or 3, so that each student can participate in solving the clues. There are 2 hint cards that each team receives, and they must decide as a team when they want to use them. "Hints" should be just that, a hint, not the solution to a clue (more on hints in chapter 2). Two of the basic principles of breakout boxes are discovery learning and problem solving. Students cannot do that if you GIVE them the answers!

If the students cannot break in with the 45 minutes allotted, then what? Do you give them extra time? No. Do you tell them where the other clues were hidden? No. Do you tell them the correct combinations to the locks? NO! Part of this learning process is having the students work through the frustration of not getting into the box. Will they always make an A? No. Will they always understand everything they do? No! Two of the lessons students need to learn is to deal with disappointment and learn from past mistakes. That may sound harsh, but students appreciate their success so much more when they have experienced failure.

After 45 minutes

It is crucial that you have some kind of "debrief" activity after the breakout box. You are going to have some students who are on cloud nine from getting in and some students who are mad at everything and everyone because they did not break in. You must allow for the frustration to have a voice so it does not end up being students yelling at each other. On the other hand, you also want the "winners" to have their moment so they don't rub anything in other students' faces. I have my students complete a "Good, Bad, Different" paper. They draw three columns and write down at least two good things, two bad things, and two things they would like to be done differently the next time we do a breakout box. The "different" column is the most informative one because it helps me to know what is working and gives me ideas of things I can improve for next time. I always tell students that if they don't tell me how they want things to be changed, that they can't complain when they stay the same!

Inside the box

Who cares about breaking in? What's inside the box that is so great? The answer is NOTHING! That is the great thing about the breakout box - the students are just excited they broke in.... they don't really care what you put in it! Some of the things I have put inside my boxes are candy (everyone's favorite), chips, juice boxes, and coupons. Coupons are the best because they don't cost anything and the students love using them. See Appendix B for the coupons I give in my classes.

Content Areas and Different Learning Styles

Many people wonder if they can use a breakout box in any subject area - whether it is a core subject or an elective. The greatest attribute of a breakout box is that it can be tailored to exactly what you are teaching in your classroom. I started using breakout boxes in elementary school math, and I am currently using them in middle school English. The flexibility that they offer is yet another positive element of the breakout box. Instead of giving a worksheet with math problems or assigning a chapter with questions in science or showing a video with questions in history or giving a passage with questions in English, use a breakout box to assess the same knowledge and more. It can be used to teach a specific skill or at the end of the unit as an assessment. You can tailor the material to your state and subject standards to ensure alignment with the district curriculum.

Breakout boxes also speak to students with many different learning styles. Kinesthetic learners, visual/spatial learners, logical learners, and interpersonal learners have their learning styles met with the breakout box. This is also a great activity for students with disabilities. The varied tasks allow students to choose which skill they want to target. Students like working in groups and are prompted to stay on task by other group members. They can move around the classroom and engage in something different from paper and pencil work at their seats (although, much of the work can be pencil and paper work!).

2

Getting Started

Where do you begin?

I believe the best way to learn how to facilitate a breakout box is to do one - that is why I wrote this book. Once you experience how the kids solve the clues and see how everything works, you will be more confident in making one of your own. The hardest thing to do is just to get started. It will not be perfect the first time - you are going to forget where you hid a clue, one of the locks won't open with the correct combination, the students may DESTROY your classroom - it's okay. Just duplicate one of the sets of clues in the book and give it a try! After your first box, then you can decide on a unit or a series of skills that you want your students to practice and start designing clues. For math, it can be as simple as a worksheet that you cut up or have the combination revealed with a black light. For science, it can be an experiment in which they have to write down the colors the liquid turns and for English, it can be your figurative language unit - just pick somewhere to start!

Supplies

As I said before, you can order complete boxes from a company that specializes in these (if your school is willing to pay for it - just Google breakout boxes). However, I will list everything you need, and you can order it from Amazon to get started with the bare minimum.

Below is the list of supplies needed for one breakout box - I highly recommend starting with at least two - and if you order in packs of two, sometimes you can save even more money! To give you an idea of how much money we are talking about, I recently looked on Amazon to price each item. These are the total costs I found:

- One box with everything but the lock box, black lights and UV markers: $52.48
- One complete box (with one of everything on the list below): $79.26
- Two boxes with everything but the lock boxes, black lights and UV markers: $89.54
- Two complete boxes with everything on the list below: $126.16

Type each item in on the list below and choose the one you want. I always get the cheapest of each item because the kids break everything! Plus, it never hurts to get extras for when something does break. You can always start with the supplies that work for you and your classroom (I saw someone using binder pencil pouches in place of tool boxes!) - just remember to adjust the time limit if you use fewer locks.

A plastic toolbox

A hasp (this is what all of the locks fit on to lock the box)

A 3-digit lock

A 4-digit lock

A word/letter lock (5 letters)

A directional lock

A key lock

OPTIONAL ITEMS:

A combination box (this is a separate box that has a 3-digit lock code)

Black light - You may also need to purchase batteries

UV marker (only one, no matter how many boxes you are buying)

Hint cards (you can make your own)

Allow me to elaborate on exactly what each of these locks are, if you do not shop for locks often. The 3- and 4- digit locks are pretty self-explanatory: the correct 3 numbers (or 4 numbers) open the lock. The word/letter lock is a lock that has letters rather than numbers. Most letter locks have five letter reels that allow you to make a plethora of different words (a word of advice - don't use words, students are GREAT at guessing words - use random letters that don't spell anything). The directional lock is a lock that requires the correct combination of up, down, right, and left to open. Directional locks can be very tricky so make sure you read the directions to reset them carefully. These locks can have an endless number of directions to open the lock and are always the students' favorite! The key lock opens with a key (shocker) and the additional combination box typically has a 3-digit lock. The chapters with the ready-made clues will explain the code to which each lock needs to be reset. All locks come with instructions on how to change the code so be familiar with the steps because you will have to reset them each time you do a new breakout box.

As for the black light and the UV marker, these are not "necessary" for the box, but are lots of fun for additional options with clues. For example, I have had a clue where students have to write the vocabulary words that match given definitions. I give the students letter blanks for the vocabulary words (ex. ___ ___ ___ ___ ___), then I put dots on one letter from each word with the UV marker so when the students put the correct word down and shine the black light on the paper, it highlights the letters needed to open the letter lock. You could do variations with numbers for a number lock as well. Most often, I put the black light in the 3-digit combination box. Once the students find the combination to the lock box, they can use the black light to help them with another clue to a different lock. Just make sure the clue for which they need the black light doesn't open the lock box.... (then they can't get in the lock box because they need the black light to solve the clue!)

A quick word on hint cards: These just need to be two cards (per team) that students can give you to receive a hint about either where a clue is located or how to solve a clue. You can type the word "hint" on paper and print it out to use. I suggest putting four on a page and laminating them, if you are able, so you can reuse them again and again.

Planning out the box

After you decide on the supplies you want to order and receive everything, you are ready to start your box. Chapter 3 has a step-by-step look at the process I go through to set-up my boxes. There is also a checklist to prepare for a box in Appendix A. I will describe an abridged version here for those of you who do not need as much direction.

Once you have decided on a unit, list the locks that you will be using:

3-digit:

4-digit:

Word:

Directional:

Key:

(Optional: 3-digit lock box)

The next step is to design the clues that you will want for each lock. There is no trick to this, and there is no magic formula. You just choose the skill you want your students to practice and design a clue around that skill. For example, if I want my students to identify types of figurative language, I could put examples on the back of a 24-piece puzzle:

1. My love is like a red, red rose (simile)
2. I was kicked out of math class for too many infractions (pun)
3. Grandpa is older than dirt (hyperbole)

The students have to assemble the puzzle and turn it over to see the clue. Now, how do each of these provide the combination for a lock? There are 6 letters in the word "simile", there are 3 letters in the word "pun", and there are 9 letters in the word "hyperbole". So this clue would open a 3-digit lock with the combination 6-3-9.

How about a math example? Put problems on a paper with a 16-square grid. Have one square labeled "start" and write in the directions "follow the path of even answers". Have 5 answers work out to be even numbers (the skill level can range from simple addition to two-step equations) and whatever the path is - left, up, right, right, down - the directional arrows will be the combination to the directional lock. This clue can be found in the 3-5 Math section.

That's how it works - you choose a skill you want students to practice and find a way to make that skill a fun clue to open a lock! If that seems like something that is way out of your comfort zone, the next several chapters are full of ready-made clues as well as many suggestions for building your own in the future. Once you get the hang of it, you will be creating your own clues in no time.

The next sections of the book are divided into grade levels and subjects so that you can assemble your own breakout box. However, the ideas for clues could be used in different subjects. So look through the other grades and subjects to keep your students from anticipating how the clues are solved.

Trying it out before investing any money:

Buying the supplies needed to implement this in your classroom costs money. I know as an educator that I do not get paid enough to buy these supplies on my own and you probably do not either. If your school is willing to scrounge up some money for you to purchase the boxes GREAT, if not, there is a way for you to at least try out how the clues will work and see how your students participate before investing a lot of money. Instead of the box with the locks, divide your board into two (or three) sections. Put "Team A" on one side and "Team B" on the other side. Write down the names of each lock (word lock, 3-digit lock, etc.) underneath each team name. Have the students bring you what they believe the correct code is when they solve a clue. If they are correct, then put a check mark next to whichever lock it goes to. If they are incorrect, tell them to keep working. Once a team has successfully "opened" all the locks, let them open up a cardboard box or make-up box or something you bring from home filled with the candy/chips/coupons. This will give you a sense of how it works before you invest money in the purchase of boxes.

I must include a disclaimer with this: Much of the excitement of the breakout box is getting to physically put in the codes and see the locks come off one-by-one. If your students are not wildly excited, please know that with the physical box, there will be much more urgency and anticipation, leading to a more engaged atmosphere.

3

Creating Your Own Box

Now you are ready to start making your own box for your students, but where do you begin? As I have said before, you have to pick a place that you want to start. If you teach middle school history, you can create a box on Westward Expansion or if you teach science, you can create a box for your students to work on the characteristics and elements of cells. You can even combine different units if you want to do a review of several concepts. Breakout boxes can be used at the beginning or in the middle of a unit, if you want your students to research information and learn as they go solving clues, or you can use it at the end of a unit to assess mastery. Although I have never tried it this way, you could also use it on a single skill that you have the students practice in different ways - it could be an excellent alternative to a worksheet or centers!

I will now walk you through choosing a unit and clue topics to see how the clues are made and how the box would be put together (for the rest of this chapter, you can insert your subject and topic for each thing we do when you are ready to make your own). There is a numbered instruction list and a timeline/checklist in Appendix A, for you to reproduce and use.

I am going to use mixed math review for our example to illustrate that you can use any skill your students are working on to create a variety of different clues.

Step 1: Determine the topics that you want to cover with your clues.

You can use multiple clues on one topic or one clue per topic, you just have to determine what you want the students to practice. It is not a bad idea to throw in review topics either - students can always use review and it is a great way to spiral teaching to keep skills fresh. For our example, I am going to use the following topics from which to build clues:

- Order of operations
- Percent of a number
- Changing decimals into fractions
- Finding a common denominator
- Multiplication (a review concept that is central to many math skills)

I chose five topics here because I plan to make a second 3-digit lock clue to open the lock box that has the black light in it. If you choose not to use the lock box, you may only need four topics (or fewer, if you are going to use the same topic for multiple clues). As I said in chapter 2, I always start by writing down the locks and then building the clues that could fit each lock. The key lock is a little different, in that it will have to be a clue that leads students to a hiding place in the room, instead of a combination to a lock. The key can also be placed in the 3-digit lock box with the black light, if you choose to use it. Keep reading to see how that clue can work.

Step 2: List the locks you will use.

3-digit:

4-digit:

Letter:

Directional:

Key:

Lock box (3-digit):

Step 3: Match the topics with the appropriate lock.

This is probably the hardest step to explain and accomplish. It becomes easier with practice, but even I still have some trial and error when trying to figure out which clue lends itself to a particular lock. Don't be afraid to change things as you go, if something isn't working, try it somewhere else. The good news is, you can force almost any clues to fit any lock - it just may take some creativity and imagination!

In my head, this is how I see the topics matching each lock:

3-digit: Converting decimals to fractions

4-digit: Order of operations

Letter: Common denominators

Directional: Percent of a number

3-digit lock box: Multiplication

Key: General

Now that I have determined which topic goes with which lock, the fun begins! I now think of how I want my students to practice a skill and I create clue that practices or assess that skill.

This does not have to be painful or difficult - you could get problems from a textbook or a worksheet…. it's all in the presentation. Here are the clues I came up with:

(3-digit lock: Convert decimals to fractions)

Find the fraction form of each decimal. Put each fraction in lowest terms.

1. 0.28   2. 4.6   3. 0.125

In UV marker (it will be invisible until the black light is shined on it) on the bottom I would write "Numerators". When the students find the correct fraction equivalent, the three numerators, will be **7-3-1....and that will be the 3-digit lock code.

(4-digit: Order of operations)

_____

$$417 + [(19 \times 3)(52\text{-}34) + 8^2 - 6]$$

_____

When the students correctly solve the problem, the solution will be **1453....and that will be the 4-digit code.

(Letter: Common denominator)

_____

Find the least common denominator for the two numbers.

1. 2 and 3   a) 5   b) 6   c) 2   d) 12
2. 4 and 6   a) 10   b) 24   c) 12   d) 6
3. 9 and 3   a) 9   b) 12   c) 3   d) 27
4. 8 and 5   a) 3   b) 13   c) 85   d) 40
5. 10 and 12   a) 10   b) 60   c) 22   d) 120

_____

**The letters of the correct answers will be the combination:
bcadb

(Directional: Percent of a number)

Find the percent of each number. Determine whether it is more than (up) 70%, less than (down) 30%,

or 31%-69% (right).

1. What percent of 52 is 13?

2. What percent of 28 is 20?

3. What percent of 67 is 31?

4. What percent of 72 is 49?

5. What percent of 95 is 70?

When the students find the correct percent of each, the combination will be: **Down, up, right, right, up

(3-digit lock box: Multiplication)

_____

1. 27	2. 56	3. 49
x 33	x 18	x 62

___ ___ ___   ___ ___ ___ ___   ___ ___ ___ ___

_____

When the students find the correct answer to each one, the underlined blank will tell them which three numbers to use to open the lock - **903

(Key: General)

You can simply hide the key somewhere in your room (I like taping it to the bottom of a trash can or desk) or you can put it inside a dictionary or textbook and create a clue to guide students there. As I said earlier, you can also put the key in the lock box with the black light. This will prevent you from having to create a separate clue for the key, but the students still have to solve the lock box clue to obtain the key.

Chapter 4: Fraction Operations

**Duplicate this and tape it up in a few places around the room, then put the key in a textbook at that chapter.

THAT'S IT!

No, really…...that's all there is to it!

<u>YOU</u> can definitely do that!!!

As you become more comfortable creating clues, you will find ways to be more creative - like putting the clue on a puzzle that the students have to put together before they can solve the clue or having a piece of paper that has another teacher's name on it, to whom they have to go see to get a clue - the possibilities are endless! Until you are ready for that, there are many pre-made boxes with clues that make up the rest of the book. Feel free to use all the clues that apply to your grade and subject, but look through all the clues. You never know what history clue could be tailored to your math skill or what language arts clue is perfect for science vocabulary also. Plus, it never hurts to do something cross curricular.... I'm sure your other content teachers would be delighted!!!

Creating Clues

1. **Choose your topics**
2. **List the locks you are using**
3. **Match topics with appropriate locks (subject to changes!)**
4. **Write clues to practice a skill**
5. **Make sure you write down the code**

4

The Day of the Show

and

Murphy's Law

Now you are ready to facilitate your first breakout box. When I said facilitate, that is exactly what I meant - the students should be doing all the work and you should be simply observing. Start the timer at the beginning, be available to provide hints when asked, stop students from trying to jimmy open the locks, and be prepared to laugh - "We're putting in the right combination, but the lock won't open!" Make sure your hints are only HINTS, it should be enough to point them in the right direction without giving the answer.

Below is an example of what I say to my students right before a breakout box begins. Feel free to adjust to what works for your class, just don't give too much away. This whole activity should be problem solving and discovery learning, so let go!

"Ladies and gentlemen - today you will be solving a series of clues to open the locks on this box. There are prizes inside that your team may enjoy, if you break in. The clues are hidden around the room. You will need to work together to get into the box - anyone not contributing, will not enjoy the prizes of the box. Any resource that you need can be used to solve the clues. Your team will receive two hints cards that you may use to receive a hint about how to solve a clue or a location of a clue. Your ENTIRE team must agree to use the hint card, so make sure you are communicating with each other.

You will have 45 minutes to solve the clues and open the locks. When 45 minutes are up, you will stop - whether you broke in or not. That is all the instruction I will provide. Best of luck and begin!"

(Make sure you tell them who is on which team and where in the room their teams' clues are hidden).

At the end of each class, you will have to put new clues out and re-lock all the locks for your next class. This may sound simple, but you might be surprised how much time it takes to actually do it. I suggest having the clues separated and ready in stacks to put into hiding places as soon as the first class finishes. I try to do this as my students complete the "Good, Bad, Different" paper. This is also the time I normally tell my students not to tell anyone in my later classes about the clues or the combinations. Students want to tell their friends about the clues and the locks, so I usually have a competition where I tell my students that the fastest group in ALL my classes to break in, receives an extra prize. This prevents many students from giving away lock combinations, but some still will. When I find that this remains a problem, I appeal to my students not to "ruin" the box for the other classes - telling other students cheats them out of the fun of the box.

Murphy's Law

Be prepared - anything and everything that can go wrong will. You forgot to hide a clue, a student broke a lock, a lock won't open, and your room is a disaster area. Don't worry, you will figure out how to deal with all of this and more. I will offer solutions to common problems that you may encounter to help you along the way.

A lock won't open

This is the most common problem and it could have several solutions: 1. Double check the code (that you wrote down) and try the lock yourself

2. Try the original lock code, in case you did not reset it correctly

3. Try one number off either way (if it was "3" try both 4 and 2) for each number of the combination

4. Offer a prize to a student if they can figure out how to open it (after the time is up)

Regardless of what you try and what works, make sure you tell the team working on that box that if they open all the other locks, they will get the prizes. If none of the options above work, you may have to cut the lock off (I have cut MANY locks!)

You forgot to hide a clue

No problem - simply look where you thought it was and give an extra copy of the clue to the team (ALWAYS keep a few extra copies of clues). Apologize to the team and, depending on how much time is left, offer them a few extra minutes to solve, since it was your mistake.

A group opens a lock without solving a clue

One of many scenarios can accompany this problem: students overhear another group saying the combination, you used a word on the letter lock and a student guessed it, you forgot to mix up the numbers when you put the lock on the box, or anything else! You have to decide the solution to this, but once someone knows the combination and the lock is off, it is very hard to try to "put it back on". If possible, I would require my students to solve the clue in order to get credit for opening the lock (sometimes difficult if they know the combination).

A clue doesn't open the lock

It is going to happen - you created a clue, it worked out in your head, but the day of the breakout box, you realize that something is missing or wrong that the students would need to solve the clue. Simple fix: apologize and guide the students through the clue (without giving away the answer, if possible). Then, think about how to fix it before the next class comes in!

The students DESTROY your room looking for hidden clues

It will happen. I almost cried the first time. I am highly organized and do not like when things are out of place or messy....and I had to let it go. No matter what I say or threaten, the kids destroy my room every time. LET THEM! They have so much fun pulling out and leafing through every single book on the shelf – and it is so funny to watch them when you know there isn't a clue there! The good news is that you can always make the students clean it up afterwards. You will still have to go behind them and do a little, but I have been able to guide mine to fixing most of what they mess up! (Good luck)

5

Technology

I would be remiss not to include a chapter about the incorporation of technology in breakout boxes. For the purposes of the book, I have not included technology clues, but there are many ways that you could (and should) include technology when you start making your own boxes. There are a few different topics that I will explore in this chapter to help you understand how technology can go hand-in-hand with the breakout box.

Digital Breakout Boxes

There are hundreds (maybe) of FREE digital Breakout Boxes that you can search and use from the internet. The great part is that they are already created for you and they are usually labeled with the subject and grade level for which they are appropriate. This is another great way to "try out" breakout boxes with your students before investing any money. The way it works is that a Google form is created that has the different locks listed (three digit, letter, directional, etc.) and students have to put all of the correct codes in and then "submit" the form to break into the box. The ones I have tried immediately reject incorrect codes, so students know right away if they are wrong. Since there is no 'physical box', you can provide prizes anyway you want. There are, however, some things to consider when choosing a digital breakout box that I will explain.

1) <u>Students prefer the physical box</u>

I put this first because I believe it is the most important thing you should know. There is something about the physical nature of the box and the removal of lock after lock to finally open the mysterious treasure that is waiting inside the breakout box that students prefer. That is not to say that digital boxes are not fun (they are!), but students overwhelmingly prefer the physical box. My students have participated in both and all but one, said they preferred the actual box to the digital one.

2) <u>No way to know the codes</u>

This is a bummer. While the ready-made clues are fantastic, there are no answer keys to know what the codes to the locks actually are. Unless you have lots of free time to go through and solve the digital boxes (call me, I have some essays you can grade), you will be blindly leading your students in the solution. Some people don't mind not knowing and even try to solve along with the students - and that is great! I just want you to be aware of what you can expect with the digital breakout boxes.

3) <u>Vastness of the internet</u>

For my students (and in my opinion), this is the biggest pitfall of the digital boxes. Literally ANYTHING could be a clue. While that sounds like a great thing, students can be chasing random rabbits down holes the entire time instead of working on the content you intended. Students can be confused about whether or not they are even working on a clue and (unless you have solved it ahead of time) you may not know yourself in order to help! Many boxes are fairly straightforward in links and clues, but several are not, so just be careful out there.

4) Requires technology to which not everyone has access

It may sound extremely enticing that, if groups are working together, you may only need two or three devices to run a digital breakout box. Unfortunately, if students have to search the internet to find the solutions to the clues, you really need one device for each student. If you do not have a device for each student, not only will it take groups longer to solve clues because they can only work on one at a time, but you will undoubtedly have students who start getting off task because they do not have something in front of them in which they are engaged. You could probably have one device for every pair of students but I would not recommend any more than that for engagement purposes.

5) Monitoring

I always like to think that I don't have this problem in my classes, but I do - sometimes, no matter how engaging the lesson and activity are, when I put technology in front of some students, they get off task. Even good students are just too tempted when they have technology in front of them - they check their grades quickly, check their email after they finish working on a clue, or (my favorite) they update their Facebook status with how much fun the breakout box is. And if that is the good students, just imagine what some of the not-as-focused students are doing instead of working.... It is much harder to monitor the digital boxes than it is to monitor the physical one.

Technology within clues

As you will discover, I have not required the use of technology with any of the clues in the following chapters. Many teachers are limited by the availability of technology to them and a wonderful aspect of breakout boxes is that you do not have to use technology if you do not want to.... but you can! I will not insult you by telling you different ways you can use technology (and that would probably fill another book!), but I will say that I have seen many creative uses of technology in breakout boxes. Using a QR code to reveal a clue or a combination is my favorite. If you are unfamiliar with QR codes, you can create your own and connect it to any clue or code that you want. The students will have to have access to a QR code reader, so keep that in mind. You can put a QR code reader app on any device ahead of time or you can allow students who have that app on their phone to use it to get the clue. The technological clue possibilities are endless and students really enjoy a mix of clue types to solve. Keep an open mind when it comes to incorporating technology in your boxes and be creative!

3rd-5th Grade Boxes

The following section is full of ready-made boxes that are appropriate for third through fifth grades. You may have to print something off for a box that is appropriate for your grade, but I tried to give you an idea of what to use and how it would work. They are separated by subject area, but you could certainly choose clues from any section to use in the same box (just make sure it opens one of each type of lock!) I purposefully tried to mix up the clues so that they were not all in the same "unit" so that you could get as many ideas as possible for how you could create clues with different units. Please know that these clues are only suggestions – if something does not work for your class, change it!

The first page is a synopsis of what the clue is about and the correct lock combination. This is the "answer key". Make sure you keep this page handy - but hidden from the students! The next page(s) are the clues separated by a line. Copy the clues for your boxes (remember to make copies for each period and a few extra, just in case). Especially the first few times you do the box, the students will struggle with the locks because they are unfamiliar with how they work. I always keep the answer key close by and tell them if they believe they have the correct combination to let me know and I will either try the lock for them or I will tell them that they need to keep working on the combination. You will have to know all the combinations to reset the locks after each class anyway. This page is also a helpful resource for lesson plans to show how the activity is linked to the curriculum (A helpful paper for when an administrator walks in!)

6

3-5 English #1

3-digit lock - Write 3 sentences. Put one in first person, one in second person, and one in third person. The order in which you write them will be the combination to the lock.

> They couldn't figure out the clues to the puzzle.
>
> (third person)
>
> I am the smartest person I know.   (first person)
>
> You can almost taste the victory.   (second person)

**The combination is 3-1-2

Directional Lock - Print off a short story you have read or an excerpt from a story you have read - I suggest <u>The Monster in the Barn,</u> by Elise Farmhouse, but any short story or even a part of a book would work (I have used and excerpt from a Harry Potter book, myself!). Cut it into five pieces (or put it on five different pages). Put arrows on the back of the story in the order you want the lock to be, so when the students put the story in the correct order, they will have the combination to the directional lock. You may want to put the strips in an envelope so they stay together!

**An example combination could be left, up, left, down, right

4-digit lock - Put the following words on index cards and mix them up:

Friendly	foggy	Be kind to others
Nervous	stormy	Love conquers all
Respectful	green	Be careful what you wish for
Spoiled	fragrant	Cherish the moment
Kind		Don't burn your bridges
		Hard work pays off
		Don't count your chickens
		before they hatch

When the students correctly group these words as character traits, setting descriptors and themes, they will have the combination to the lock by how many are in each group. The combination will be least to greatest.

**The combination is 4-5-7

Word - Print off 5 short myths or fables (more than one per page, if you can fit them to save paper). Number them from 1-5. Put one letter of the word "myths" or "fable" in the top corner (M on #1, Y on #2, etc.) with marker (or UV marker, if using a black light).

**The combination is either M-Y-T-H-S or F-A-B-L-E

Key lock - Tape definitions of the same word up around the room (ex. Perseverance). Put the key in the dictionary on the page where the definition is found. Make sure you have a dictionary and a key for each group/box.

**THESE ARE THE CLUES! Duplicate these sheets and make copies for each group (Ex. If you have two groups per class, then you will need two copies of <u>each clue</u> for each class). Cut each one on the solid line. Do not write on the clue which lock it opens…. that's what they have to figure out!

3-5 English #1

From which perspective is each sentence written?

They couldn't figure out the clues to the puzzle.

I am the smartest person I know.

You can almost taste the victory.

Group the like words together.

The combination is least to greatest.

Don't burn your bridges   Kind   Green

Friendly   Don't count your chickens before they hatch

Foggy   Stormy   Spoiled

Love conquers all   Be careful what you wish for

Respectful   Be kind to others   Fragrant

Cherish the moment   Hard work pays off

Don't count your chickens before they hatch

Perseverance - steady persistence in a course of action, a purpose, a state, etc., especially in spite of difficulties, obstacles, or discouragement. (www.dictionary.com)

3-5 English #2

Word - Create a crossword with vocabulary words for your class (you can use as few as 5 words). Search the internet for a free crossword creator and print! Either highlight the letters for the words you want to be the combination OR highlight them with UV marker.

Possible vocabulary words:

Appropriate

Envy

Plentiful

Humble

Conclude

**Possible combination with these words: C-R-I-Y-H

3-digit lock - Have a text with multiple choice questions. The questions I wrote go with The Lifting Stone, by Anne Eliot Crompton. The correct multiple choice answers are letters that spell out numbers (t-w-o, s-i-x, o-n-e)

**The combination is 2-6-1

4-digit lock - Put four prefixes and/or suffixes on a paper and write directions for students to match them with their meanings. Number the meanings of each one.

The combination will be the order that the <u>meanings </u>match the <u>prefixes/suffixes</u>.

*The combination is 3-4-1-2

Key lock - I like to make my students write for some clues. You can pick whatever assignment you want for them to write - I like to have mine write thesis statements or introduction paragraph, maybe even descriptions of something. The clue can be the writing prompt and when everyone in the group turns it in, you can give them the key.

Directional lock - Provide students with sentences that have one word omitted. The omitted word is a homophone and the students have to put the correctly spelled word in to complete the sentence. The correct word should have the arrow for the combination next to it (you will have to draw in the arrows).

**A possible combination is down, up, right, down up

**THESE ARE THE CLUES! Duplicate these sheets and make copies for each group (Ex. If you have two groups per class, then you will need two copies of <u>each clue</u> for each class). Cut each one on the solid line. Do not write on the clue which lock it opens…. that's what they have to figure out!

3-5 English #2

Match the prefix or suffix with the correct meaning.

-ic   1. without

trans-   2. before

-less   3. having a characteristic of

pre-   4. across

Place the correct word in each sentence.

1. I am going _____ the store.   Two   To   Too

2. Animals like playing outside _____.   Two   To   Too

3. There are _____ choices for lunch today. Two   To   Too

4. _____ school colors are blue and gold.

        There   Their   They're

5. We used to live over _____.   There   Their   They're

Everyone in your group must write a paragraph about why recycling is important to help take care of the earth. You must have a main idea sentence and a minimum of three supporting details. Turn all papers in to your teacher for the next clue.

Answer each question from the story for a lock combination.

1. What does the word "homely" mean in the first paragraph?
    k) Like a home

    t) Not very pretty

    s) Humble

    o) Beautiful

2. Why doesn't Mandy Jane want Wealthy to marry?

    d) She will be lonely without her

    h) She secretly does not like her

    e) She wants to marry Moses Fiske

    w) She knows she cannot do the housework that Wealthy

        does

3. What does the word "enormous" mean in the fifth paragraph?

    o) Very big

    r) Very small

    n) Very flat

    u) Very round

4. Why did Wealthy "fret" when Mr. Hatch, Mr. Bushrod, and Mr. Fish tried to move the stone?

    e) She was afraid they would hurt themselves

    v) She didn't want to ever get married

    s) She didn't want to marry any of those men

    t) She hoped that someone would move it so she could leave

5. What type of figurative language is the phrase, "That stone sits where she is."?

   a) Simile

   e) Metaphor

   i) Personification

   o) Hyperbole

6. On page 2, what does "I beat a path to the kitchen" mean?

   n) She hit the dirt on the way to the kitchen

   h) She beat her horse in a race to the kitchen

   x) She took a shortcut to the kitchen

   r) She ran very fast to the kitchen

7. Why did Mandy Jane tell Moses how to move the stone?

   f) She felt bad for Wealthy

   g) She felt bad for Moses

   t) He tricked her into telling him

   o) She wanted to prove she was clever

8. On page 3, what does the word "nudged" mean?

    n) Gently pushed

    h) Violently hit

    i) Quickly kicked

    e) Softly blew

9. Why did Moses gulp when Papa told him he was so clever?

    o) He got rain in his mouth

    e) He knew that Mandy Jane was the clever one

    n) He didn't know if Papa was going to change his mind

        about the marriage

    t) He was nervous to see Wealthy

7

3-5 Math #1

3-digit lock - Provide three pictures or three names of polygons. The combination will be the number of sides of each shape.

**The combination is 7-4-9

4-digit lock - Find the volume of a figure (regular or irregular). Choose a figure that is appropriate for your grade and difficulty level. Don't be afraid to let it be a 3-digit answer with a zero in front!

**Possible combination is 0-9-0-0

Directional - Give students five decimal numbers. For each one, have them decide whether it would be rounded up (arrow up) or stay the same (arrow down). (You could do different place values for each one to make it more challenging)

**The combination is up, down, down, up, down

Word - Give students 5 measurement conversions. Show what the amount is in one measurement (ex. 5 L) and then put another measurement (ex. 500 _L) and have them write the first letter of the new unit.

**The combination is c-d-k-m-h

Key lock - tape the word "calculate" with the definition around the room. Put the key in a math book in the glossary on the page where the word can be found.

**THESE ARE THE CLUES! Duplicate these sheets and make copies for each group (Ex. If you have two groups per class, then you will need two copies of <u>each clue</u> for each class). Cut each one on the solid line. Do not write on the clue which lock it opens…. that's what they have to figure out!

3-5 Math #1

Heptagon

Quadrilateral

Nonagon

Decide whether each number would be rounded up (up) or stays the same (down) based on the given place value.

1. Hundredths   65.906
2. Ones   234.49
3. Thousandths   0.972
4. Tens   785.1
5. Hundred thousand   9,047,188

Write the missing letter for the measurement conversion.

1. 5 L = 500 __L

2. 65 mm = .65 __m

3. 320 hg = 32 __g

4. 8.07 L = 8,070 __L

5. 90 dag = 9 __g

<u>**Calculate**</u> - to determine or ascertain by mathematical methods. (www.dictionary.com)

3-5 Math #2

3-digit lock - Provide pictures of different types of triangles – six acute, two right, and four obtuse. Paper clip the triangles together or put them in an envelope and let students group them together. The number in each group is the combination.

**The combination is 6-2-4

Directional - Divide a paper into 16 blocks. Give a starting point and have the students solve problems. The combination will follow the path of odd numbers. (You can do any types of numbers – even, odd, prime, composite, imaginary, negative...be creative!)

**The combination is up, up, right, down, right

Word - Scramble 5 vocabulary words from the current unit. Give the definition and number of letters. Underline one letter from each word. The underlined letters are the combination. Possible vocabulary words can be found on the next page, but you could use ANY words from your unit or even words you haven't covered but want the students to look up!

Possible vocabulary words:

Estimate

Place value

Equivalent

Perimeter

Regroup

**Possible combination with these words: S-A-V-E-R

(I know this spells a word and I said not to do that, but since it is unrelated to the vocabulary words, I think it is safe to use it. Feel free to change it, if you disagree!!)

4-digit lock - Provide four numbers written out into words. Have students identify different place values for each number.

**The combination is 2-9-3-0

Key lock - Hide the key (tape to a calculator or the bottom of a trash can!)

THESE ARE THE CLUES! Duplicate these sheets and make copies for each group (Ex. If you have two groups per class, then you will need two copies of <u>each clue</u> for each class). Cut each one on the solid line. Do not write on the clue which lock it opens…. that's what they have to figure out!

3-5 Math #2

Put the triangles in groups of acute, right, and obtuse.

1. Taiseemt   __ __ __ __ __ __ __ __

2. Calep luvae   __ __ __ __ __   __ __ __ __ __

3. Veealuqint   __ __ __ __ __ __ __ __ __

4. Ripeteme   __ __ __ __ __ __ __ __

5. Progure   __ __ __ __ __ __ __

Tens place - Eight hundred-thousand two hundred ten

Ones place - Six thousand two hundred fifty-nine

Tenths place - Four hundred ninety-seven and thirty-one

hundredths

Hundreds place - Thirty-five thousand sixty-one

Follow the path of odd numbers.

594 / 33	225 / 9	487 + 694	1058 - 269
762 - 48	17 x 23	771 − 685	103 x 37
45 x 22	**START**	612 / 17	544 + 988
468 / 9	16 x 24	78 + 204	601 - 93

8

3-5 Science #1

3-digit lock - Provide picture or names of animals from three different groups (mammals, fish, reptiles). The number of animals that are in each group is the combination.

**The combination is 4-7-2

Directional - Put animal/plant names or pictures that belong in a food web. Have students put them in the order they would be for a food web (you may have to tell them which one to start with so they get the right order for the combination). Put arrows on the back of each plant or animal that will provide the combination when put in the correct order.

**Possible combination could be: left, down, left, right, up

4-digit lock - Put the names of four elements around the room. Write the words "periodic table" at the bottom of each paper. The atomic number of the element will be the combination.

**The combination is 9-1-6-4

Word lock - Create a crossword from a vocabulary unit. Search the internet for a free crossword creator, enter your words and definitions and print! Highlight 5 letters (or highlight with a UV marker) that will be the combination.

Possible vocabulary words:

1. Carnivore
2. Habitat
3. Erosion
4. Organism
5. Taiga

**Possible combination for these words: V-A-N-G-I

Key lock - Hide the keys somewhere in the room (Under the trashcan or in a first aid kit is always fun!)

**THESE ARE THE CLUES! Duplicate these sheets and make copies for each group (Ex. If you have two groups per class, then you will need two copies of <u>each clue</u> for each class). Cut each one on the solid line. Do not write on the clue which lock it opens…. that's what they have to figure out!

3-5 Science #1

Put the animals in like groups - mammals, birds and amphibians.

polar bear   parrot   alligator

snake   toucan   koala

dolphin   chameleon   sea lion

Put the following in the order they would be in a food web.

Frog   Eagle   Flower

Snake   Butterfly

---

1. Oxygen
Periodic Table

2. Hydrogen
Periodic Table

3. Carbon
Periodic Table

4. Helium
Periodic Table

3-5 Science #2

Directional - Provide a picture of the water cycle. Omit 5 words. The students will fill in the words and when listed alphabetically, the arrow direction that goes with the word will be the combination.

**The combination is down, up, up, right, down

Word - Have the students read a paragraph about conducting experiments. Misspell 5 important vocabulary words by one letter. The correct letter for each misspelled word is the combination.

Reseerch = research

Problen = problem

Hipothesis = hypothesis

Exberiment = experiment

Resultz = results

**The combination is A-M-Y-P-S

3-digit lock - List examples (or provide pictures) of types of energy. The number of examples in each group is the combination.

**The combination is 6-4-2

4-digit lock - Scramble vocabulary words and provide letter blanks and definitions. Highlight (or UV marker) letters that spell out numbers (Nine, one, two)

Mantle	**N**
Habitat	**I**
Dependence	**N**
Luster	**E**
Erosion	**O**
Mineral	**N**
Core	**E**
Vertebrate	**T**
Weathering	**W**
Adaptation	**O**

**The combination is 9-1-2

Key lock - Put papers up around the room that say "periodic table". Put the key in a science book on the page with a periodic table.

**THESE ARE THE CLUES! Duplicate these sheets and make copies for each group (Ex. If you have two groups per class, then you will need two copies of <u>each clue</u> for each class). Cut each one on the solid line. Do not write on the clue which lock it opens…. that's what they have to figure out!

3-5 Science #2

The Water Cycle

1. Percolation
2. Evaporation
3. Plant uptake
4. Transportation
5. Surface flow

There are several steps that are necessary to properly conduct an experiment. The first step is to reseerch a topic that you want to know more about or prove something about. Then, you have to determine a problem with the topic that you want to conduct an experiment to explore. Next, you will need to formulate a hipothesis - this is your educated guess about how the experiment will turn out. Now you will need to conduct your exberiment to test whether your educated guess was right or wrong. Finally, you must analyze your resultz to determine the facts about the topic and the experiment.

Categorize each example as chemical energy, potential energy or kinetic energy.

Battery	a car at the top of a hill
Burning campfire	opening a shaken soda
Swinging on a swing	an apple in a tree
Boiling water	a rolling wagon
A pulled rubber band	photosynthesis
Gasoline in a car	a spring in a pinball machine

___ ___ ___ ___ ___ ___ the portion of the earth between the crust and the core

___ ___ ___ ___ ___ ___ ___ the natural environment of an organism

___ ___ ___ ___ ___ ___ ___ ___ ___ ___ the state of relying on or needing someone or something for aid, support, or the like

___ ___ ___ ___ ___ ___ the state or quality of shining by reflecting light

___ ___ ___ ___ ___ ___ ___ the process by which the surface of the earth is worn away by the action of water, glaciers, wind, waves, etc.

___ ___ ___ ___ ___ ___ ___ any of a class of substances occurring in nature; any substance that is neither animal nor vegetable

___ ___ ___ ___ the central layer of the Earth

___ ___ ___ ___ ___ ___ ___ ___ ___ ___ having a backbone or spinal column

___ ___ ___ ___ ___ ___ ___ ___ ___ ___ the various mechanical and chemical processes that cause exposed rock to decompose

___ ___ ___ ___ ___ ___ ___ ___ ___ ___ the ability of a species to survive in a particular ecological niche, especially because of alterations of behavior

(www.dictionary.com)

Periodic Table

Periodic Table

Periodic Table

9

3-5 History #1

4-digit lock - List presidents (or vice presidents) and have students find what number president they were.

(Washington = 1, etc.) The numbers put together are the combination.

**The combination is 9-28-6

Directional - pick a decade/century. List five events. Students must find when the events occurred - an earlier century (left), the same century (down), or a later century (right).

Cotton gin invented	1793
Transcontinental railroad completed	1863
Queen Elizabeth I ruled England	1533
Fall of the Berlin Wall	1989
American Civil War	1861

**The combination is left, down, left, right, down

3-digit lock - Have students find the years that several events took place. Have them add and subtract each year successively. The final difference will be the combination.

The year Marcus Aurelius was born = 121

+

The year the Wright brothers made the first flight = 1903

-

The year the Crusades began = 1095

-

The year Attila the Hun crossed the Rhine into Gaul = 451

**The combination is 4-7-8

Word lock - Provide five vocabulary words #1-5. Put matching definitions in a second column with letters a-e. When the word and definition are correctly matched, the order will provide the combination.

**The combination is D-C-E-A-B

Key lock - Tape the word "time" with its definition around the room. Hide the key in a dictionary on the page where the word "time" can be found.

**THESE ARE THE CLUES! Duplicate these sheets and make copies for each group (Ex. If you have two groups per class, then you will need two copies of <u>each clue</u> for each class). Cut each one on the solid line. Do not write on the clue which lock it opens.... that's what they have to figure out!

3-5 History #1

William Henry Harrison

Woodrow Wilson

John Quincy Adams

Decide whether the events listed happened in an earlier century (left), the same century (down), or a later century (right).

<u>1800s</u>

Cotton gin invented

Transcontinental railroad completed

Queen Elizabeth I ruled England

American Civil War

Fall of the Berlin Wall

The year Marcus Aurelius was born

+

The year the Wright brothers made the first flight

-

The year the Crusades began

-

The year Attila the Hun crossed the Rhine into Gaul

_____ _____ _____

1. Customs

    a. the branch of government having the power to make laws

2. Migration

    b. the production of crops, livestock or poultry

3. Pioneer

    c. to go from one place to another

4. Legislature

    d. a groups pattern of habitual activity

5. Agriculture

    e. a person who is among those who first enter or settle a region

(www.dictionary.com)

Time - indefinite and continuous duration regarded as that in which event succeed one another.

(www.dictionary.com)

3-5 History #2

Word lock - Provide a world map. Put numbers on each continent/ocean for students to name. Highlight (or UV marker) letters in the words that will be the combination.

Possible locations to number:

In**d**ian Ocean

South Amer**i**ca

A**f**rica

Mediter**r**anean Sea

Asi**a**

**The combination is D-I-F-R-A

Directional lock - List famous discoveries or wonders of the world. Provide a world map. Have students identify whether the discover happened north or south of the equator (arrows up or down).

**The combination is up, up, down, up, down

4-digit lock - List four events from your unit. Provide blanks for the year date next to each (ex. _ _ _ _). Highlight one number from each event. This will be the combination.

**The combination is 5-7-3-8

3-digit lock - Provide events that happened in three different decades. Have the students group the events by decade. The number of events in each decade is the combination.

**The combination is 7-4-3

Key lock - Hide the key somewhere in the room (I like to use the side of a window!)

**THESE ARE THE CLUES! Duplicate these sheets and make copies for each group (Ex. If you have two groups per class, then you will need two copies of <u>each clue</u> for each class). Cut each one on the solid line. Do not write on the clue which lock it opens…. that's what they have to figure out!

3-5 History #2

Name each continent or ocean labeled on the map.

1. ___ ___ ___ ___ ___ ___   ___ ___ ___ ___ ___
2. ___ ___ ___ ___ ___   ___ ___ ___ ___ ___ ___ ___
3. ___ ___ ___ ___ ___ ___
4. ___ ___ ___ ___ ___ ___ ___ ___ ___ ___ ___ ___ ___

   ___ ___ ___
5. ___ ___ ___ ___

Determine whether each famous landmark lies north (up) or south (down) of the equator.

1. Stonehenge
2. Great pyramid of Giza
3. Christ the Redeemer
4. Lighthouse of Alexandria
5. Great Barrier Reef

In which year did each event take place?

Magna Carta ___ ___ ___ ___

Hundred Years War begins ___ ___ ___ ___

Black Death ___ ___ ___ ___

War of the Roses ends ___ ___ ___ ___

Put each event in the correct decade:

1920s   **1940s**   **1960s**

Jackie Robinson joins Dodgers   Bay of Pigs

Japanese attack Pearl Harbor   Scopes trial

Women gained right to vote   State of Israel founded

Martin Luther King "I have a Dream" speech   Prohibition

Harlem renaissance   First Olympic winter games

Lindbergh flies solo over Atlantic   JFK assassinated

King Tut's tomb is discovered   FDR elected to third term

Jackie Robinson joins Dodgers

6th-8th Grade Boxes

The following section is full of ready-made boxes that are appropriate for sixth through eighth grades. They are separated by subject area, but you could certainly choose clues from any section to use in the same box (just make sure it opens one of each type of lock!). For some subjects, I tried to mix up the clues so that you could get as many ideas as possible for how you could create clues in different units and others I stuck with one unit. Please know that these clues are only suggestions – if something does not work for your class, change it!

The first page is a synopsis of what the clue is about and what the correct lock combination is. This is the "answer key". Make sure you keep this page handy - but hidden from the students! Especially the first few times you do the box, the students will struggle with the locks because they are unfamiliar with how they work. I always keep the answer key close by and tell them if they believe they have the correct combination to let me know and I will either try the lock for them or I will tell them that they need to keep working on the combination. You will have to know all the combinations to reset the locks after each class anyway. This page is also a helpful resource for lesson plans to show how the activity is linked to the curriculum (A helpful page when an administrator walks in!)

10

6-8 Math #1

4-digit lock: Provide two of the three sides of right triangles. Have the students solve for the missing side using the Pythagorean theorem. You can also provide pictures, if your students need a visual.

**The combination is 5-2-5-8

3-digit lock: Give students the two figures' coordinates and have them figure out the translation right and then down. (If you want to draw the figures on a coordinate plane, you can; or provide a coordinate plane on which the students can graph the figures!).

**The combination is 1-5-7

Letter: Have the students find the positive slopes using the provided points. You can provide the change in slope formula - or don't, if you are assessing that skill.

**The combination is A-D-F-H-I

Directional: The students will find the volume of each figure using the information provided. The combination will be the arrows associated with the figures that have a volume less than 4,000.

**The combination is up, down, left, up, down

Key: Hide the key somewhere in your room! (In a textbook or on the board with the "No Name" papers…. someone may find their work!)

**THESE ARE THE CLUES! Duplicate these sheets and make copies for each group (Ex. If you have two groups per class, then you will need two copies of <u>each clue</u> for each class). Cut each one on the solid line. Do not write on the clue which lock it opens…. that's what they have to figure out!

6-8 Math #1

Solve for the missing side of each right triangle.

1. B = 12, C = 13   2. A = 6, C = 10   3. A = 15, B = 20

How far was the figure translated?

Original figure: (-9,8) (-2,8) (-9,3) (-2,3)

Translated figure: (6,-4) (13,-4) (6,-9) (13,-9)

Positive slopes

A. (0,4) (3,5)   F. (2,6) (11,10)
B. (1,1) (0,3)   G. (3,5) (7,1)
C. (7,7) (9,2)   H. (0,0) (4,9)
D. (4,6) (2,5)   I. (1,8) (5,4)
E. (8,3) (0,7)   J. (10,2) (2,10)

Find the volumes less than 4,000.

1. Rectangular prism L=21, W=14, H=8   Up
2. Cylinder r=9, h=13   Down
3. Rectangular prism L=22, W=17, H= 12   Right
4. Cube s=8   Left
5. Cone r=11, H=21   Up
6. Cylinder r=12, H=9   Right
7. Cube s=16   Left
8. Pyramid B=324, H=15   Down

6-8 Math #2

Letter: The students will solve each one-step equation to find the answers which are odd numbers.

**The combination is Q-R-T-M-V

Directional: The students will solve each linear equation and decide if the answer is more than 10 (up) or less than 10 (down).

**The combination is up, down, down, up, down

3-digit: The students will solve the percent/unit rate problem to find the number in the tenths place to create the combination. Caution: For the last problem, it says "what percent", so the number in the tenths place of the percent will be zero!

**The combination is 4-5-0

4-digit: The students will use measures of central tendencies to find the code. They must put the code in the order: mean, median, mode and then range.

**The combination is 6-7-8-7

3-digit lock box: This is a word problem dealing with area. Feel free to draw a picture for the students, if you think they need one.

**The combination is 3-8-4

Key: Put papers up around the room that say "Calculation is KEY in math" and hide the key with the calculators.

**THESE ARE THE CLUES! Duplicate these sheets and make copies for each group (Ex. If you have two groups per class, then you will need two copies of <u>each clue</u> for each class). Cut each one on the solid line. Do not write on the clue which lock it opens….that's what they have to figure out!

6-8 Math #2

1. Q – 12 = 25

2. 10 = Z + 6

3. R / 7 = 7

4. T – 19 = 32

5. 24 = 4C

6. 18 = A / 3

7. 11 = M - 4

8. 8X = 96

9. S + 17 = 65

10. V / 5 = 9

More (up) or Less (down) than 10?

1. One less than two times a number equals 45.
2. Three times a number minus seven equals that number minus seventeen.
3. Twelve minus three times a number minus two times the same number equals negative three.
4. Eighteen more than negative two times a number equals nine less than negative one times the number.
5. Two times a number increased by one equals thirty-six more than negative three times the number.

Tenths place

15% of 36

Unit rate: $94.50 for 7

What % of 52 is 13?

Mean, Median, Mode and Range

3, 8, 3, 7, 6, 7, 5, 8, 4, 8, 9, 2, 8

A picture frame has a length of 26 in and a width of 18 in. If the frame is one inch on each side, what will be the area of the picture inside the frame?

Calculation is KEY in math.

11

6-8 History #1

4-digit: This is the date of the Louisiana purchase doubled (since the Louisiana purchase doubled the size of the United States!)

**The combination is 3-6-0-6

3-digit: The students have to identify the number associated with each question related to Westward expansion.

**The combination is 4-1-2

Letter: The students have to identify each person/place/thing associated with Westward Expansion.

President at the beginning - Thomas Jefferson

Belief - manifest destiny

1844 president - James K. Polk

1846 slave state – Texas

1855 fight - Bleeding Kansas.

**The combination is F-E-K-X-G

Directional - Students identify whether each place is north or south of the 36 30 parallel.

1. Gadsden - south
2. Oregon - north
3. Maine - north
4. Mexico - south
5. Illinois - north

**The combination is down, up, up, down, up

Key - Post the words "Popular Sovereignty" around the room. Put the key in a textbook in the glossary where the term can be found.

**THESE ARE THE CLUES! Duplicate these sheets and make copies for each group (Ex. If you have two groups per class, then you will need two copies of <u>each clue</u> for each class). Cut each one on the solid line. Do not write on the clue which lock it opens…. that's what they have to figure out!

6-8 History #1

Louisiana Purchase did this to the size of America. Do that to the date of the purchase.

1. How many parts did Kentucky Senator Henry Clay's compromise have?

2. Approximately how many square miles did the 1848 Treaty of Guadelupe Hidalgo add to the US?

3. The third digit of the latitudinal parallel associated with the Missouri Compromise.

Initial westward expansion president:

— — — — — —   — — — — — — — — —

Belief that westward expansion was justified:

— — — — — — — —   — — — — — — — —

1844 president:

— — — — —   — —   — — — — —

1846 slave state that joined the Union:

— — — — —

1855 name of civil war fight in Kansas:

— — — — — — — —   — — — — — —

North or South of the 36 30 Parallel?

1. 1853 purchase

2. 1846 land treaty

3. 1820 state that entered the Union as a free state

4. 1846 declaration of war against this country by President Polk

5. State from which senator Stephen A. Douglas hailed

Popular Sovereignty

6-8 History #2

3-digit: Students will complete the last word of each invention during the Industrial Revolution. The number of letters in each missing word will be the combination

(ex: spinning _____ - the correct answer is "jenny", which has 5 letters, so the first number in the combination is 5)

**The combination is 5-4-6

4 digit: Students have to find the correct year for each event. Once they find the dates, they will have to find the black light (in the lock box) that will tell them to add all of the dates together to get the combination to the lock. If you do not use the black light, simply provide four blanks for each event and highlight the correct number blank for the code.

**The combination is 7-3-6-6

Directional: The students will find each place and decide whether it is north (up), south (down), east (right), or west (left) from Promontory Point.

**The combination is down, right, left, left, right

Letter: The students must match the terms together. The letter of the matching term, in order, will provide the combination.

**The combination is C-E-A-B-D

3-digit lock box: The students must decipher the Morse code of numbers to find the combination.

**The combination is 3-8-1

**THESE ARE THE CLUES! Duplicate these sheets and make copies for each group (Ex. If you have two groups per class, then you will need two copies of <u>each clue</u> for each class). Cut each one on the solid line. Do not write on the clue which lock it opens.... that's what they have to figure out!

6-8 History #2

Industrial Revolution Inventions

Spinning _____

Power _____

Steam _____

Adam Smith published <u>The Wealth of Nations</u>

The Luddite Rebellion began

Alexander Graham Bell invented the telephone

The Wright brothers made the first successful airplane flight

---

Where is each place in relation to the final meeting point of the two sides of the transcontinental railroad?

Cape Horn

Omaha, Nebraska

Sacramento, California

Pacific Ocean

New York

---

1. Stock _____   a. free

2. Communist _____   b. unions

3. _____ enterprise   c. exchange

4. Trade _____   d. child

5. _____ labor   e. manifesto

· · · __ __

__ __ __ · ·

· __ __ __ __

12

6-8 Science #1

Directional: Students will decide if each statement about photosynthesis is true (up) or false (down).

**The combination is up, up, down, up, down

Letter: Students have to figure out which parts match which body system. When they figure this out, the number of parts that are in the system tell the students which position the first letter belongs in for the lock (ex: **R**espiratory system has <u>one</u> part listed - lungs, so the **FIRST** letter of the lock will be R).

**The combination is R-N-C-D-S

4-digit: The students have to determine which number the planet is from the sun.

**The combination is 6-2-8-3

3-digit: The students must complete the Punnett square and add the probability of each trait together to get the combination. Write the word "ADD" in UV marker next to the % questions at the bottom.

**The combination is 2-2-5

3-digit lock box: The students identify the number of each law of motion.

**The combination is 3-1-2

**THESE ARE THE CLUES! Duplicate these sheets and make copies for each group (Ex. If you have two groups per class, then you will need two copies of <u>each clue</u> for each class). Cut each one on the solid line. Do not write on the clue which lock it opens…. that's what they have to figure out!

6-8 Science #1

True (up)   or   **False** (down) ?

Chlorophyll absorbs the sun's energy.

Oxygen is released from the plant's leaves into the atmosphere.

Chloroplasts produce hydrogen.

Water is absorbed through the plant's roots.

Glucose is released through the stomata.

Group the following parts with their appropriate body system:

Digestive system   **N**ervous system   **S**keletal system

Respiratory system   **C**irculatory system

Spinal cord	Heart	Tibia
Lungs	Gall bladder	Metacarpals
Humerus	Brain	Capillaries
Pancreas	Sternum	Esophagus
Arteries	Small intestines	Clavicle

Saturn   Venus   Neptune   Earth

Create and solve a Punnett square for each trait.

Bb and bb   B=brown eyes, b=blue eyes

HH and Hh   H=brown hair, h=blonde hair

Tt and Tt   T=tall, t=short

% chance of blue eyes?

% chance of brown hair?

% chance of being tall?

For every action there is an equal and opposite reaction.

An object will remain at rest or in uniform motion unless acted upon by an external force.

Force is equal to the change in momentum per change in time: $F=m * a$

6-8 Science #2

Directional: Students will decide whether each thing can be found in a plant cell (right), animal cell (left), both (up) or neither (down).

**The combination is up, right, down, up, left

Letter: Students will identify each vocabulary word and use the underlined letter to find the combination.

1. Speed
2. Distance
3. Time
4. Velocity
5. Mass

**The combination is E-C-M-O-S

4-digit: Students will put the ecosystem organizational levels in order from largest to smallest.

**The combination is 2-1-7-5

3-digit: Students will answer multiple choice questions about natural disasters. The correct letter of each multiple choice response will spell out a number (ex. #1=T, #2=W, #3=O, those three answers spell out the number TWO, which will be the first digit of the combination).

**The combination is 2-6-1

**THESE ARE THE CLUES! Duplicate these sheets and make copies for each group (Ex. If you have two groups per class, then you will need two copies of <u>each clue</u> for each class). Cut each one on the solid line. Do not write on the clue which lock it opens…. that's what they have to figure out!

6-8 Science #2

Which of the following belong in plant cells (right), animal cells (left), both (up), or neither (down)?

Mitochondria

Cell wall

Anaphylaxis

Nucleus

Cilia

___ ___ ___ ___ ___ - rapidity in movement

___ ___ ___ ___ ___ ___ ___ ___ - the amount of space between two things

___ ___ ___ ___ - indefinite, continuous duration in which events succeed one another

___ ___ ___ ___ ___ ___ ___ ___ - the time rate of change of position of a body in a specified direction

___ ___ ___ ___ - a large coherent body of matter without a definite shape

(www.dictionary.com)

Put the following organizational levels in order from largest to smallest.

Ecosystem (7)

Population (2)

Biome (5)

Community (1)

Find the correct response to each question.

Which is NOT a stage of a volcano?

  r) active s) dormant t) sedentary f) extinct

Friction from the plates in the Earth's crust causes:

  w) earthquakes i) landslides   o) floods h) tsunamis

What is the name of a porous, volcanic rock formed during eruptions?

  x) putrid r) petrified   u) petra   o) pumice

What causes tsunamis?

  e) the gravitational pulls of the sun and moon

  f) residual hurricane winds

  s) underwater earthquakes and volcanoes

  o) tidal waves

What is the difference between lava and magma?

    o) there is no difference

    i) magma is inside the volcano, lava is outside

    e) magma is solid, lava is liquid

    n) magma is white, lava is red

Which is true of The Ring of Fire?

    t) located in the Pacific Ocean

    u) accounts for 90% of all earthquakes

    i) a famous Johnny Cash song

    x) all of the above

The size of an earthquake is called its:

    o) magnitude   n) intensity   w) scaling   e) range

The scale used to measure earthquakes is called the:

    h) Seismic scale   n) Richter scale

    e) Amplitude scale   i) Intensity scale

Landslides cause:

n) snowmelt   o) stream erosion

x) earthquakes   e) all of these

13

6-8 English #1

Letter: Print out a poem (I like Haiku....it puzzles the students!) Highlight five random letters in the poem with the black light.

**Possible combination: H-B-S-O-M

Directional: Students must identify the birthplace of each poet in relation to your state. (Caution: depending on which state you live in, the combination could be imprecise – change the directional arrows to match wherever you live).

**Possible combination if you live in the south: up, right, down, up, left

4-digit: Print out (or provide a book/internet with) 3 poems - I used 'Ozymandias' by Percy Bysshe Shelley, 'I Carry Your Heart' by E.E. Cummings, and 'I Wandered Lonely As A Cloud' by William Wordsworth. Provide multiple choice questions that, when answered correctly, spell out four numbers (the first three correct answers are S, I, X - so the first number in the combination is 6).

**The combination is 6-1-0-2

3-digit: Write down three types of poems for students to define. Put a plus or minus sign in between each one. The students will either add or subtract page numbers on which each word can be found in your classroom dictionary to come up with the correct combination - make sure it equals a 3-digit number!

**The combination is whatever 3-digit number you come up with!

Key: Hide the key somewhere in your room!

**THESE ARE THE CLUES! Duplicate these sheets and make copies for each group (Ex. If you have two groups per class, then you will need two copies of <u>each clue</u> for each class). Cut each one on the solid line. Do not write on the clue which lock it opens…. that's what they have to figure out!

6-8 English #1

Find the birthplace of each poet in relation to our state

(north, south, east or west).

Emily Dickinson

Percy Shelley

Pablo Neruda

Edgar Allen Poe

Robert Hass

Ozymandias

1. What does "visage" mean?

Q. hand

R. body

S. face

T. head

2. Which is an example of personification?

H. "whose frown and wrinkled lip"

I. "and the heart that fed"

J. "legs of stone stand in the desert"

K. "and sneer of cold command"

3. Who is Ozymandias?

U. a traveler

V. an Egyptian pharaoh

W. an important historical figure

X. a long forgotten ruler

I Carry Your Heart

   1.   Why does the poet use parentheses?

   T. those words are meant directly to his love

   U. those are words he is thinking but does not say

   V. those words are literary devices

   W. those words are secrets

2. Which is an example of figurative language?

   D. "i want no world"

   E. "i carry your heart with me"

   F. "the root of the root"

   G. "the deepest secret nobody knows"

3. What is the tone of the poem?

   K. worrying

   L. ridiculing

   M. smothering

   N. adoring

I Wandered Lonely As A Cloud

1. In stanza 1, what is "fluttering and dancing in the breeze"?

   R. clouds

   S. trees

   T. daffodils

   U. crowd

2. What word supports the meaning of the word "jocund" to be cheerful?

   V. danced

   W. gay

   X. sparkling

   Y. gazed

3. Which is an example of figurative language?

   L. "a cloud that floats on high"

   M. "stars that shine"

   N. "the sparkling leaves"

   O. "the waves beside them danced"

Define each type of poetry using the blue school dictionary:

Ode -

Limerick -

Haiku -

6-8 English #2

4-digit: Students must identify which part of argumentative writing is described. The number of letters in each correct response will be the combination (ex: CLAIM has 5 letters, so the first number in the combination is 5).

1. Claim
2. Rebuttal
3. Backing
4. Warrant

**The combination is 5-8-7-7

Directional: Print of a reading passage (at your students' lexile) that has multiple choice questions with it. Cut up the questions and just give one question with the passage. The students have to bring you the correct answer to receive the next question. Put a directional arrow on the back of each question you give the students.

**Possible combination: right, up, left, down, left

Letter: Give the students a prompt for which they must write an introductory paragraph. When every student in the group has turned it into you, highlight five letters from different paragraphs in the UV marker and return all the paragraphs to the group.

**Possible combination: D-A-P-Y-R

3-digit: Provide the introductory paragraph and the text evidence for students. Put numbers on the back of each piece of text evidence. You can print off the article or let students look it up, if you have computers. The three correct pieces of text evidence will be the combination.

**The combination is 2-4-9

3-digit lock box: Students must decide in which person the sentence is written. When they correctly identify the point of view, that will be the combination.

**The combination is 2-1-3

**THESE ARE THE CLUES! Duplicate these sheets and make copies for each group (Ex. If you have two groups per class, then you will need two copies of <u>each clue</u> for each class). Cut each one on the solid line. Do not write on the clue which lock it opens.... that's what they have to figure out!

6-8 English #2

---

1. The thesis - your side of the argument

2. A "comeback" for why the claim is wrong and you are right

3. Statistics, studies, numbers or professional testimonies

4. Your reason for using a particular piece of evidence

Everyone on the team must read the passage. When you are finished, one person may answer the first question. Bring the question with your answer to the teacher. You will receive an envelope with the second question. A DIFFERENT PERSON must answer the next question and bring the answer to the teacher to receive the next question. You will continue having DIFFERENT PEOPLE answer each question until all questions are answered.

---

*EVERY PERSON ON YOUR TEAM must write an introduction paragraph for the following prompt. The introduction MUST INCLUDE a hook, bleeders and a thesis. When you finish your paragraph, bring it to the teacher. When everyone has turned one in, you will receive the code to the lock.

In a growing Age of Technology, people are relying on computers to do more and more to help save time. New technology is available that would grade student essays for teachers. Should computers be used to grade student essays?

"Where there is a will, there is a way." This familiar quote means that if a person wants something badly enough, they will find a way to make it happen. If humans want to prevent mass extinction, they must find a way to make it happen. The article, "People are causing a mass extinction on Earth; some try to stop it", from Scientific American, offers many ways that humans can aid in conservation and prevent further extinction.

Find the THREE pieces of text evidence that support the thesis.

1. Fish can bounce back when we stop overfishing.

2. Endangered species may need to be moved to help them survive the changing climate.

3. In the most extreme case new animals could be brought in. They could replace animals that have gone extinct.

4. The animals and plants of the Amazon rainforest have benefitted from Brazil's efforts to stop deforestation.

5. For example, European sailors ate their way through the Indian Ocean of Mauritius. They killed off the dodo bird and the local turtle species.

6. Advances in genetics and biology could make it possible.

7. Based on an estimate in Nature in 2011, we have a century or two before our actions assure a mass extinction.

8. Bringing back extinct species could cause problems, as could replacing extinct animals with similar ones to restore ecosystems.

9. Paleo ecologists found that 20 out of 21 large mammals in India - from leopards to muntjac deer - have survived there for the past 100,000 years.

_____

You want to make sure your essay uses formal writing style.

I always remove contractions to add to the formal tone.

Some people are unaware that formal writing should always be in third person.

_____

14

Electives

I wanted to include a chapter for the always under-appreciated elective classes. I taught an elective (AVID) for three years and I know what it is like to never get the love and attention that the core content areas always receive. That having been said, I am by no means qualified to suggest content for clues in either of the following subjects.... but here goes nothing!

This chapter includes suggestions ONLY for clues to a music and a P.E. box. I know that there is probably limited technology available in these rooms, so I have tried to keep it "technology light". As for the clues, I cannot give you a combination because it is dependent upon your clue choices and space. Hopefully, this simply gives you some ideas of how you could incorporate this and then you can email me your own box ideas that have been wildly successful!

Music

Letter: Put 5 music notes on a staff. The name of each note will create the code. You could also have students write the names of all of the notes on a sheet of paper and highlight five of them with a UV marker. Only when a group correctly names ALL of the notes on the page, can you give them the black light.

*To increase difficulty, make a quarter note = 1 letter and a half note = 2 letters.

3-digit: Play a CD during the box with famous classical pieces (maybe some that you have discussed before or allow the students a way to look them up). The number in the titles will be the combination - ex. Concerto #5, so 5 would be the first number in the combination.

Or

Describe different voice parts (the highest female voice part - soprano etc.) Once students figure out the voice part described, the number of letters in the voice part will be the combination.

1. The lowest male voice part (bass - 4)
2. The highest female voice part (soprano - 7)
3. The middle male voice part (baritone - 8)

4-digit: List four composers (perhaps some that you have discussed or studied) and ask for their birthdates. Have the students add or subtract (or a combination) to come up with a 4-digit number.

Or

List instruments in an orchestra and the number of letters in the instrument will be the combination.

1. Trombone (8)
2. Viola (5)
3. Oboe (4)
4. Bassoon (7)

Directional: Ask students where certain notes are in relation to a note on solfeggio (ex -"fa", then list other notes and have students decide if they are up or down from fa).

Or

Ask students where certain keys are in relation to a certain key on the piano.

Or

Ask students about 5 musical periods (baroque, classical, etc.) in history. Pick an arbitrary date (ex. 1742) and ask students if the musical time period occurred before (left), in the same time as (down), or after (right) that date.

Key: List a musical key around the room. Tape the key to that note on the piano.

Or

Hide the key somewhere in the room

P.E.

3-digit: Have the students add/multiply the number of steps it takes to go around the gym to the number of steps it takes to go lengthwise and the number of steps it takes to go widthwise (I would have them check with me after they "measure" each one so I can tell them if they need to count again - you may even have them round to the nearest zero, to help with approximation).

Letter: Give the students a picture of the Olympic rings - and NOTHING else. The combination will be the first letter of each ring color.

**The combination is B-Y-B-G-R

4-digit: If you can get 4 teachers to agree (or school staff) .... Give the students a piece of paper with 4 teachers/staff members' names on it. The students have to find each of those people to get a number for the lock.

**Possible combination: 7-3-5-0

Directional: Give the students a long list of physical activities to complete. Make sure five of the activities have an arrow (up, down, left, right) as part of the instructions. The order of the arrows will be the combination.

*You could also put the arrows at the end of the list with the UV marker and require everyone on the team to finish all the activities before you give them the black light.

Key: Tape the key to the top of the basketball "key" with black tape. You could tape up pictures of a basketball key around the gym as well.

Appendix A

Suggested Timeline and Checklist for Making a Box

1 week before

_____ Make sure you have all supplies (boxes,

locks, batteries, etc.)

_____ Start thinking of clues

3 days before

_____ Finish and finalize clues (make sure you

have one for each lock!)

_____ Make your "answer key"

2 days before

_____ Type up all clues and print out

_____ Cut apart different clues

_____ Gather prizes and/or coupons for the box

1 day before

_____Set all locks (the first time, you may want

to do this sooner in case something goes

wrong and you have to go buy another lock)

_____ Lock up box with prizes

_____Hide clues for your first class

The Day of the Show!

_____ Pull up the timer on your computer

_____ Relax and enjoy!

Creating Clues

1. Choose your topics
2. List the locks you are using
3. Match topics with appropriate locks (subject to changes!)
4. Write clues to practice a skill
5. Make sure you write down the code

Choose Topics

1.

2.

3.

4.

5.

Clues

3-digit:

4-digit:

Letter:

Directional:

Key:

Lock box (3-digit):

Appendix B

Coupons!

Sit Anywhere!

Switch seats with another student or sit in an empty seat for the day!

Name_____

Date_____

Sit at Mrs. Johnson's desk!

Sit at Mrs. Johnson's desk for the day (Just don't move anything!)

Name_____

Date_____

Put your feet up!

Mrs. Johnson will bring you a chair to prop your feet up on during class! (what?!?!?)

Name_____

Date_____

Cup of cocoa!

Mrs. Johnson will make you a cup of cocoa to enjoy during class! (how cool is that?!)

Name_____

Date_____

Choose your group!

Choose your own group or your partner on a day we work in groups!

Name_____

Date_____

Chew Mrs. Johnson's gum!

Mrs. Johnson will give you a piece of gum to chew during class! (I must be crazy?!)

Name_____

Date_____

Piece of candy!

Get a piece of candy from Mrs. Johnson's stash! (Stay away from the Reece's - I think they're old, anyway)

Name_____

Date_____

Teacher's assistant!

Pass out papers, collect items, sit at Mrs. Johnson's desk - you're almost the teacher!

Name_____

Date_____

Replace a low grade!

Replace your lowest minor grade with a 100! (No tests, quizzes or book reports!!)

Name_____

Date_____

Exam bonus points!

Good for 10 extra points added on to your exam grade! (You deserve it ;)

Name_____

Date_____

Free Homework 100!

You've earned it! Take a day off and enjoy no homework!!

Name_____

Date_____

Listen while you work!

Listen to music during in-class work time - just make sure to bring your earbuds!

Name_____

Date_____

References

Crompton, A. E. & Sewall, M. (1978). *The lifting stone.* New York: Holiday House.

Dictionary.com (n.d.). Various vocabulary words. Retrieved June 29, 2017, from http://www.dictionary.com/

Hall, Nancy (Ed). Newton's Laws of Motion (n.d.). Retrieved June 29, 2017, from http:www.grc.nasa.gov/www/k-12/airplane/newton.html

History.com Staff. (2010). Transcontinental Railroad. Retrieved June 29, 2017, from http://www.history.com/topics/inventions/transcontinental-railroad

History.com Staff. (2010). Westward Expansion. Retrieved June 29, 2017, from http://www.history.com/topics/westward-expansion

Opinion: People are causing a mass extinction on Earth; some try to stop it. (n.d.). Retrieved June 29th, 2017, from https://newsela.com/articles/sixth-mass-extinction/id/5277/

Wicker, C. (n.d.). Retrieved June 29, 2017, from http://www.weatherwizkids.com/weather-volcano.htm

Farnham, E. (2012). *The Monster in the Barn.* Asheville, N.C.: United Writers Press

About the Author

Holly Johnson has spent twelve years as a teacher. While she is a master math teacher, she has taught multiple subjects to students in grades four through twelve.

Johnson received her bachelor's degree from Baylor University and is currently pursuing her master's degree in education. She is a proud army wife and mother of two. Johnson is certified to teach in two different states and currently lives in Hattiesburg, Mississippi. For more information about her work, she invites you to contact her at breakoutboxobsessed@gmail.com.

Printed in Great Britain
by Amazon

11673662R00088